PETER,
I KNOW
THIS To GOOD L---.

THE 59-SECOND MIND MAP

by
Richard Konieczka
with Pat Armstrong

HARA
PUBLISHING

Seattle, WA

Published by
Hara Publishing
P. O. Box 19732
Seattle, WA 98109

ISBN: 1-883697-38-7
Library of Congress Number: 94-073803

CONTENTS

Contents

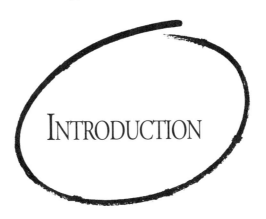

INTRODUCTION

Why another book about mind mapping, when it was already introduced by Tony Buzan in *Use Both Sides Of Your Brain*? The style used by Tony Buzan is quite different than the methods you'll find as you read on. His format resembles sentence diagramming, kind of a root and branch system with items written on lines that branch off in different directions.

The method described in the following pages goes one step further from the rigidity of lists and traditional outlining. Encircling thoughts and tying them together as they occur feels (to us at least) more natural, closer to the way our brains organize information. Buzan's book covers mind mapping in a single chapter as part of a larger premise. We've taken a great idea, modified it and extended it. Give it a try, and see what it does for you.

For those readers disposed to using the computer extensively, Inspiration Software, Inc. has a software called Inspiration that is very user friendly for creating Mind Maps on the computer. A free demo and idea book can be obtained by calling (800) 877-4292 or writing to:

Inspiration Software
2920 SW Dolph Court Suite 3
Portland, OR 97219

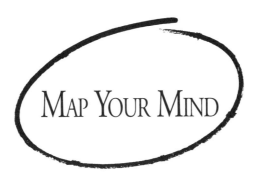

MAP YOUR MIND

Our culture is really big on lists. In addition to making lists for shopping, things to do, things to remember, etc., we publish lists as news—best dressed, top Ten's, top Forty, and the Fortune 500, to name just a few. Sometimes it seems we need lists of lists to remember to look at them. Lists can be an efficient method of storing and ranking information, as long as the items are already in some sort of linear order (alphabetical, numerical, by zip code, etc.), or priority is obvious.

Unfortunately our minds don't work that way. And to prove it, just try to write down the most important things you have to do today, in their order of importance—within the next sixty seconds. Now, how many items did you miss and how many need to be shifted up or down on your list? Our minds tend to free associate, to group thoughts according to their relationships to one another, rather than proceed in the linear fashion of outlining we are taught in grammar school.

Sticky notes, as shown on the cover, have provided a partial solution by allowing us to unload our brains of random tidbits of information, but their abuse can add to the clutter and confusion.

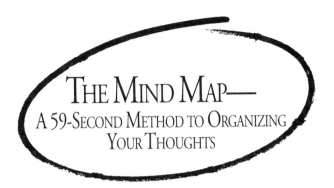

THE MIND MAP—
A 59-SECOND METHOD TO ORGANIZING YOUR THOUGHTS

Mind mapping is easy because it works on paper the way your thought processes naturally occur. The basic concept can be learned and applied instantly. It can be used to organize your goals for the next five years, objectives for the next quarter, strategies for this week and things to do today, and each "list" will take a minute or so to complete.

The key is to relax, and allow your thoughts to flow without censorship or judgment.

My first experience of mind mapping occurred as I was writing an article for a magazine. The task before me was of considerable magnitude, requiring reams of information to be condensed into a few hundred words. Like most people, my usual style was to write a draft of the article without an outline.

Long before I completed my initial draft, it became obvious that I was creating a confusing and disorganized stream of contradictory and unrelated information. Because this project was on a tight schedule, there was no time to continue in my "trial and error" mode. Recalling the wisdom of my fourth-grade English teacher, I created a classic outline to impose some sort of order and hopefully bring a little clarity to the process.

It looked exactly like this:

    I. Introduction

    II. Body

    III. Conclusion

This brilliant organizational strategy did little to illuminate the task at hand, so I cast about for another approach.

MY FIRST MIND MAP

In a state of mild desperation, I started to jot down all the information specific to the article. As my random notes took form on the page, I noticed that I had unconsciously arranged them in a sort of hub-and-spoke fashion. With the article as the central focus, I continued, adding elements until the entire project was laid out in front of me…like this:

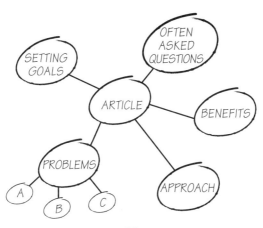

Once the content was displayed where I could see it all at a glance, it was a simple process to sequence the information and write the article in a logical and coherent fashion.

All there is to remember about mind mapping is as simple as 1, 2, 3.

1) Jot down the central theme.
2) Write words or phrases that relate to the central theme, circling and connecting them to the center as you go.
3) Use your own style

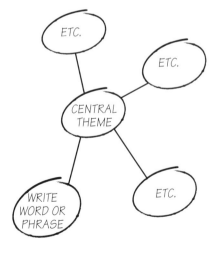

The method described is my own personal preference, and not a set of rules. The important thing is to create a mind map that is comfortable, reflecting our own natural style and thought patterns.

Some themes for mind mapping are patently obvious...things to do, shopping lists and such, but there is no situation that cannot benefit from a mind map as long as two criteria are met: 1) The central issue should be of some importance to us, and 2) there is some sense of urgency. Our central idea could range from planning a vacation to reorganizing a company—the important thing is to write down everything that is in our minds to build a visual foundation of the task at hand. And the best way to do it is the same way our minds work, using free association.

THE WORDS

It's not necessary to be expansive. As a matter of fact, the simpler the better. Most mind maps are for personal use, although they can be helpful as informal status reports and memos. As long as the information communicates the message intended, to yourself or associates, jargon and acronyms are perfectly acceptable and perhaps more effective.

MAKING CIRCLES

The shape isn't important and no points are awarded for neatness. The only problem that we may encounter here is if we draw circles first, then try to fill them with words. Writing outside the circles can cause visual confusion, making it difficult to get the big picture at a glance. Editing thoughts to fit in a pre-determined space impedes the free flow of ideas. So write first, then draw. My preference is clouds or balloons, because I can tailor the size and shape to fit the content, but any closed graphic will work just fine.

CONNECTING OUR THOUGHTS

Connecting each cloud or circle to the central theme reinforces the visual relationship, and I find that using a pen, rather than a pencil, makes a bolder statement, adding to emphasis and recall. The mind map is a working tool. Add, cross out, and indicate elements of a task completed. Amending a mind map is usually the result of additional information, and can provide an audit trail of thought processes which may be useful later.

YOUR FIRST MIND MAP

Put a central theme in the middle of the page, circle it, then surround it with related ideas. Pick a topic related to leisure-time goals, such as exercise, family activities, personal development or whatever. Use a separate piece of paper if you wish—just make sure you start in the center. I generally make all of my mind maps on an $8^1/2$ X 11, except for small ones such as those used for grocery shopping or errands. (If you want to do a different topic, go ahead...no one's watching.)

Now is the time to start mind mapping. As Nike says, "Just do it."

THE IMPORTANCE OF PERSONAL EXPERIENCE

If you didn't make a mind map, find something to write with and do it now. If you're like me and have a hard time writing in a book, just grab a piece of paper. It is essential to give yourself a personal experience of mind mapping, otherwise continued reading will just sound like so much hype, and may just build resistance to using this valuable tool. It isn't important to get it right, but it is important to try it for yourself so you can relate to the rest of this section from a position of personal experience.

If you are one of those rare individuals who suffer from "mind map block," now is the time to get past it.

Some people have a meaningful mind map experience the first time, thinking, "Where has this been all my life?" Others think they might have missed something, because the process is so simple. Some make a list and convert it to a mind map format, and can't see the difference between a Mind Map and conventional list-making. The concept of mind mapping is deceptively simple, and phenomenal benefits are derived from its use. We don't always have to pay an exorbitant sum to receive a remarkable value, and in the case of mind mapping, very little investment is required.

What does mind mapping do, and how does it do it? Following are some comments I have received during my seminars.

It's a Visual Tool. Mind mapping provides a visual reference that engages brain functions not stimulated by an outline format.

It's The Big Picture. Mind mapping is a visual overview that enables us to review all facets of a topic without getting bogged down in detail during the brainstorming process.

It's Fast. If it takes more than one or two minutes to complete a mind map, something's amiss. If it takes longer, it may be too early to map the topic, or the wrong topic to map. Then I find it handy to take it as far as the information flows, and come back to it later. If the information doesn't flow, there may be another topic on my mind more important than the one I have chosen.

It's Easy. Mind maps are not a struggle. They just collect information already in our minds, and help us to assemble it on paper. Once it's there, it's easy to reference as we proceed to the conclusion of a project.

It Makes Prioritizing and Sequencing Simple. Once all the pieces of a puzzle are in front of us, arranging them in the right fit is an easy matter. When we have mind mapped a situation or project, it's a straightforward process to prioritize and sequence the individual elements.

It Fosters Retention. When we do a mind map, we are grouping relevant pieces of information together in a visual and conceptual association. The process stimulates memory retention, and it's possible to refer to mind maps that are months, even years old and recall details that would be otherwise unavailable to us.

It's Flexible. Add, subtract or modify information. There's plenty of white space in a mind map and sequencing is left until last, so there is no "investment" in the way a mind map is arranged on the page.

It's an Expansive System. As the elements of a mind map flow out of our thought processes, each item suggests others, triggering all the associations we hold on the topic. Before long we have a comprehensive map of all the relevant information. ·

It's a Creative Process. The associations we jot down often lead to others that would not have occurred to us in a less visual approach. Mind maps allow us to see relationships developing between previously unrelated elements.

It Depicts Sequence. Items can be placed together or joined by lines into like groups. We can use arrows to indicate time or direction. Interfaces can be identified at a glance.

It's Energizing. It's easy to get started, to overcome the inertia that accompanies more formal systems of organizing, and once we are over the first hurdle the process itself generates more energy to proceed. Once set in motion, the creative flow of ideas is a powerful force.

It's Relaxing. It may seem like a paradox, but tension surrounding most situations is due to inactivity, rather than activity. Any writer will tell you that the first word is the hardest. This is because of the infinite choices available. Which direction do we travel? Without a mind map it seems we need to organize our thoughts to write them down to organize them. With a mind map, we write first, then the organization comes naturally. And getting started on a mind map is the easiest of all, since all we have to do is write down the topic—the next thought will arrive before the ink is dry on the first.

It's Complete. A mind map is always finished, but never has to be. When the flow of information on a mind map is done for the moment, you can be pretty sure you haven't left anything out. As new data is acquired, or new relationships suggest themselves, information can be added without trouble. A mind map is a living document, always in a state of progress.

It Disciplines Our Thinking. The frequent use of mind maps helps discipline our thinking. When we are aware of how we organize and store information in mind map form, we can monitor our thinking to provide a visual representation of communication content. It may also prompt questions to help fill in missing pieces.

It's Not For Emergency Use Only. We don't have to wait until things get out of hand to get organized, although mind maps are invaluable tools to use in a state of crisis. In a stress situation we all tend to redouble our efforts while losing sight of our objective. A mind map will always restore focus to what's necessary and what's next.

AUTHORED
AT
30,000 FEET

My second experience of mind mapping came on a three-week vacation, island-hopping in the Caribbean and visiting friends and relatives across the country. Combining an overdue vacation with my desire to write a book seemed to make a lot of sense. The endeavor was reasonable, since the book was to be a guide to investing based on a seminar I had delivered over fifty times. Because all the content was to come from existing information, the main thrust of the project was organizational.

I began on the red-eye to Atlanta. I was able to mind map the entire content of the book on two 8 ½ x 11 pages (the only time one of my maps has gone over a single page, but after all, this was an entire book). A single cloud included anything from a complete chapter to bits of data. I only needed to note what was top-of-mind at this point, because each reference provided all the recall necessary to expand later.

After all the pieces of information were displayed in front of me, it was very straightforward to group them under logical chapter headings. While mind mapping bits of information, I created a potpourri chapter under the heading "Most Frequently Asked Questions" for anything that didn't easily relate to already grouped ideas. Any fact could be stated as a response to a question, creating a relationship between seemingly unconnected, but necessary items. I then made a mind map of each chapter and commenced to write. By the time we touched down I had written the first chapter and knew everything else I was going to say in the book!

I began a second chapter while sunning on a Martinique beach in the midst of a number of increasing distractions (the beaches of Martinique seem to be full of them). It was decided then and there to complete the project up in the air, so to speak. Thirty-some hours of flight time remained on my city-hopping vacation, time which could be put to excellent use writing, and with a minimum of distraction. I returned home with a fully edited manuscript, having enlisted fellow passengers as proofreaders. The fact that I completed the book entirely while flying provided some inspiration for its title, *Investing In These Turbulent Times* (a time-dated book on investing).

Taking a three-week vacation is a great way to test time management skills. When I returned, the backlog seemed insurmountable, and included some twenty margin calls that needed to be made immediately. A margin call is made to clients to advise them of significant investment loss, with even limited recovery based on spending more money...with no guarantee of success. While there may be less desirable tasks than making margin calls, none come immediately to mind.

A mind map was then constructed with the theme "Catch Up." A simplified version looked like the example on the following page.

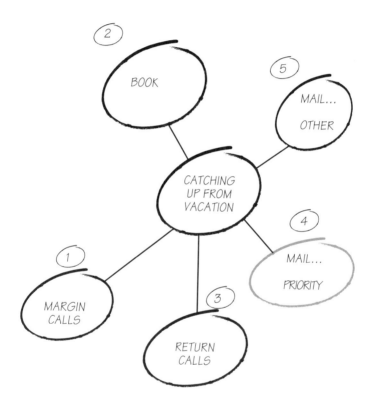

THERE'S NO MORE TIME... OR ANY LESS, FOR THAT MATTER

All the time there ever was has already been created for us. We can only use it moment by moment. Classic time management theory suggests listing everything we have to do and prioritizing these in groups of A's, B's and C's, then attempt to complete the A's. Although I did not realize it at the time, my mind map constituted a to-do list of my A priorities. The beauty of the mind map approach is that we don't have to deal with B's and C's until the A's are out of the way. And by the time we are ready to address the B's, they have already reached A status—prime mind map material—or are no longer. We don't waste time writing and re-writing items whose time is later or not at all.

KEEPING THE BALLS IN THE AIR

For us, the mind map is the answer to the venerable time management question, "What is the best use of my time—right now?" A consultant once advised Andrew Carnegie to list his most important "to-do" and complete it before going on to the next one. That may have been great advice for avoiding procrastination in the 1900's, but the pace of the '90's ill-affords most of us that luxury. Interruptions, meetings, the telephone, etc., require us to juggle several activities simultaneously. A mind map tells us at a glance what comes first and what's next, allowing us to optimize the trade-offs in time, location, personnel and resources to best focus our energies.

For example, my post-vacation mind map showed the twenty margin calls as top priority, so I began them first. On seven of the 20 calls I placed, I connected with the people I needed to speak to and left messages for the rest. Circumstances did not allow completion of this activity. Throughout the day, six calls were returned. They did not constitute an intrusion on my time, because they were top priority on my mind map. By the next day my number one priority was down to seven calls, and I repeated the procedure.

REALLY
BOOKING

Immediately after making my 20 margin calls and leaving messages where necessary, I returned to my mind map priority two, the book. The book action only required a phone call and placing the manuscript in the mail to the publisher—hardly any time at all.

Returning calls was just a repeat of the margin call format, and I reached about one-third of the people, leaving messages for the rest. Mail sorting was next, and it was easy to maintain focus, even though calls were returned throughout the day. Junk mail was tossed and periodicals were stacked for after five o'clock attention. (It was interesting to note how a three-week aging process simplified mail handling, but it's not a method I would recommend without good reason.)

I had been back in the office just under two days and I was down to my last A priority, which was now a manageable stack of correspondence.

I seem to suffer from jet lag whenever I travel, even when no time zones are crossed, and it used to require a week—sometimes two—before I felt completely on top of things again. This time my mind map really kept me on track. A glance always provided the comfort that the most important items were receiving the attention due, and there was no nagging guilt over what else was not being done at the moment.

This generated a sense of relaxed attention that allowed productivity to soar while keeping stress to a minimum—"No, everything could not be done at once and—yes, everything that could be done was being done." It was an exhilarating feeling, an awareness and relationship with time I had not known previously. It allowed 100% efficiency and proficiency, and by Wednesday, it was business as usual. Others who have taken my seminars have experienced the same phenomenon. One small business owner, who often worked until 10 pm, now regularly leaves the office at five, without guilt or worry.

One time-management expert once said "why work harder only to fail, when less work, systematically applied, will yield not only success, but more free time as well." So many time management systems stress the handling of details more efficiently so we can handle more details. Mind mapping concerns itself with the effectiveness of our activities so we don't get bogged down in the details.

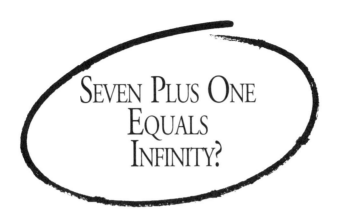

SEVEN PLUS ONE EQUALS INFINITY?

In his book *Watership Down,* Richard Adams depicts his rabbit characters as considering any number over six too large to count. For humans, the number seems to be seven. We all easily commit to memory a goodly number of 7-digit phone numbers, but recall, and even dialing, of numbers coupled with an area code requires a considerable increase in concentration.

In *Positioning: The Battle For Your Mind,* Trout and Ries point out that according to advertising research, we all carry a maximum of seven "positions" at a conscious level, and the most effective advertising triggers a response to one of those existing positions.

Mind mapping tends to reflect this phenomenon. Mind maps rarely contain more than seven main topics or clouds, while each topic can be subdivided into two or more subtopics, and that total seldom surpasses seven. In many cases it is not even necessary to write down subtopics, because the main reference tends to trigger the secondary information. This keeps a mind map simple and uncluttered, which facilitates its use as a communications vehicle when discussing a family of projects or activities.

If we were to generate a mind map with seven main topics and break each main topic into five subtopics, we can see how easy it is to access the 35 total elements of information and their relationships by merely glancing at them. Compare this experience with trying to work from a list of 35 items. Listing requires us to read and re-read to access items relevant to our immediate need for information.

The mind map increases our ability to reference up to five times the amount of information usually immediately available to us. Given the intensity of today's business environment, it's certainly a tool worth using.

Son of a Mind Map

The topics of one mind map will frequently spawn other maps. These new maps or extensions of old ones can be generated on the same mind map (if there is room) or on another sheet of paper.

While mapping out *Investing in These Turbulent Times*, I used a single letter-size map for each chapter. One associate of mine, a freelance designer, keeps all his mind maps in a steno pad, mapping projects, assignments, billing and administrative duties. Another method reported to me is using 3x5 index cards for topics and subtopics and arranging them like puzzle pieces to fit specific applications. Mind mapping is truly a system adaptable to an infinite number of personal styles.

It's time for another test. It's an easy one because there are no wrong answers. On a scale of one through ten, rate your assertiveness level, with 10 being very assertive and 1 being not very assertive. Since everyone's level of assertiveness varies with a given situation, average yours across the board.

Not Very Assertive   Very Assertive

1   2   3   4   5   6   7   8   9   10

The thought processes of relatively assertive individuals tend to be random in nature, while the thinking patterns of less assertive individuals lean toward sequential.

All individuals possess each mode of thinking to some degree, and without this balance, it would be impossible to function.

Random thought processes come under the heading of multi-dimensional thinking, while sequential styles are referred to as linear or time-ordered. On the plus side, those with high levels of assertiveness—thinking multi-dimensionally—seem to be able to "shift gears" rapidly. They skip from task to task and appear to be able to juggle several projects at once, handling responsibilities with a high degree of intuition.

Less assertive individuals—thinking sequentially—take a more logical, reflective approach to most situations. They analyze tasks at hand, performing them to completion with a high degree of attention to detail.

Our tendencies to favor one thought process over the other can be quite strong, and influential across the entire range of our activities. Compare the two approaches in the purchase and assembly of an outdoor barbecue. A random thinker might opt to pay a service charge for an assembled unit or buy a floor model, even if it has minor flaws. If that option is not available, assembly will commence immediately, using the instructions as a last-resort guide to undo a mistake. The random-thinking individual's intuitive sense and experiential learning style are the operating forces here.

Sequentially-oriented individuals would rarely consider purchasing a floor model, and find a good deal of satisfaction in the detail of assembly. They frequently follow the logical process of reading the instructions in their entirety, taking an inventory of parts to ensure the uninterrupted completion of the task, and may even group parts into the illustrated sub-assemblies before picking up a screwdriver. As one might expect, more multi-dimensional thinkers tend to end up in management, where assertive behavior and the ability to shift from one duty to another are requisites for success.

On the other hand, linear thinkers lean toward engineering, the sciences, accounting and financial controlling, where logic and attention to detail are essential requirements.

I once observed an extremely sequential individual give a sophisticated camera as a Christmas present to a random-oriented relative. As the recipient eagerly began to explore the various knobs and buttons, he was admonished to "read the directions twice before you touch it!"

Regardless of your persuasion a mind map melds multi-dimensional and linear thinking into a single exercise. By providing a reference and reminder of the different aspects of a project or situation, it gives intuitive individuals an overview of the details necessary to complete their tasks. For the detail-oriented, a mind map visually depicts the probable and possible relationships between elements that may not be readily discernible when taken in sequence.

In short, a mind map makes managers better managers by helping them pay attention to detail, and makes analytical types better analyzers by increasing awareness of the big picture.

SOME MIND MAP APPLICATIONS

The example on the following page is by no means an exhaustive list of mind map uses, but can serve as a reminder for some of the ones we have already discussed, and may trigger some ideas of your own. Everyone has areas in their lives that can benefit from mind mapping, but the application of a mind map to one subject by a certain individual may be totally inappropriate for the person working in the next office. Use your mind maps where they work best for you.

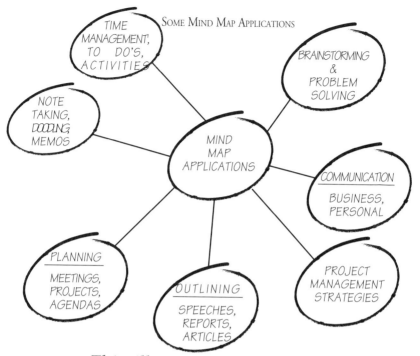

This illustration in itself is a great example of how a mind map compresses information without compromising availability. All the essentials are communicated without resorting to grammatically correct sentences or even phrases. When we create a mind map, our minds fill in the adjectives and the verbs, and continue to do so each time we refer to it.

Although a mind map may feel rather skeletal to the uninitiated, once one has an understanding of its function it becomes the quintessential shorthand, ideally suited to our fast-paced environment.

RETENTION
AND
RECALL

As previously noted, we all think in mind maps, but we don't always commit our thoughts to paper in the same fashion. Many writers use a variation of mind mapping called "clustering" to organize their thoughts, and even those who seem to "just write" without formal or informal notation, have already mentally mapped their topics.

Whenever we read a book or article, or process any other form of communication, we can take advantage of mind map principles. Any concept can be mind mapped, whether for the purpose of communicating it or understanding it. For example, mind mapping the content of a book we read will result in a set of notes that may be quite similar to those of the author prior to writing it. Making a grocery mind map and arranging the items roughly according to store location, i.e., dairy, frozen and produce, will not only enhance memory, it can also save mileage on the cart.

This mind mapping in reverse can enhance our understanding and retention by stimulating associations of the ideas in context. And our mind map is an excellent source of notes for later review.

I once received this thank you note from a participant in one of my mind mapping seminars:

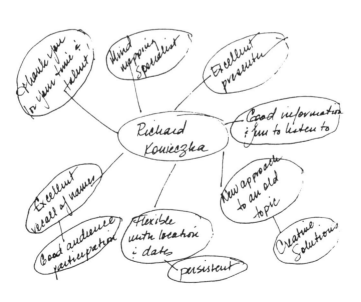

This note communicated more to me than ever would have been possible in a letter, no matter how many pages it contained.

Granted, my position as an instructor of mind mapping contributed to my joy at seeing this tool understood and put to use, but even to someone with no exposure to the mind map concept, there is no mistaking the message.

Another realization came with this note. I use to believe that mind maps were to be used for me, by me and on me, but when I saw how complete the communication was with the thank you note, I realized how effective mind maps could be in communication. If the note had been put into the form of a letter it could easily have taken a whole page what with prepositions, verbs, and transitions without changing the message. As a result, I have been much more enthusiastic about encouraging people to share their mind maps with others, thus saving time and improving communication.

ONE LAST LOOK

After you have mapped and completed a complex project, or written a lengthy report, it sometimes pays to mind map it again. Just as the mapping is an expansive process, so is writing, managing and creating. A second mind map, generated when we feel we have finished an activity, will accomplish two functions. It will confirm that we have exhausted our thoughts or resources and provide a comfortable "that's as good as it gets" feeling, or bring to the surface additional relationships and information that came to light during the process—items that were not apparent when we generated our initial mind map—allowing us to improve the final product and ensure that additions are free from confusion and redundancy. The use of different colors can highlight sequence or relationships. For example, all of the items circled in red, could represent engineering items and those in blue, production, etc.

A final mind map also leaves an accurate audit trail of the creative process for future reference.

MIND MAPPING IN THE WILDERNESS

The ideal working and communicating environment is one where everyone mind maps. If you are in a position to create policy, you might be interested in a company-wide seminar taught by yours truly...you might suggest that this book is required reading if employees wish to stay in the company fast lane...or you might hire an in-house communications coordinator to implement a mind map system specific to your needs, utilizing the principles contained herein. Short of these suggestions, mind mapping can be used effectively by any number of individuals in any organization—at any level of group involvement.

A LONE RANGER... BUT NOT FOR LONG

Everyone is a manager, whether we manage our personal output independently, or coordinate the efforts of a group. Mind mapping is an ideal method of representing the formal goals and objectives of any staff.

As a manager, the visual format of a mind map is ideal for condensing information into an easily understood global overview of projects, assignments and their relationships. Once we expose associates, subordinates and superiors to a faster, easier method of communication, it often becomes the preferred form of communication. Even if mind mapping doesn't spread like wildfire, the benefits realized by the individuals who use it contribute to their increased individual efficiency.

As individual members of a group, we can use mind mapping as a bottom-up (subordinate to manager) or top-down (manager to subordinate) method to communicate our understanding of supervisory goals and objectives. In many cases, changes in procedure and priority are issued as if in a vacuum, and analysis of repercussions is fragmentary and disjointed, if it occurs at all. Even the most ineffective communicator will find a mind map easy to understand. Sharing from the bottom up or from the top down via a mind map can illustrate beyond a doubt how new projects or workload shifts will affect the work-in-progress picture.

A mind map can't help but expose inappropriate short-term reactions to changing situations, and create an opportunity for an alternative response—long before the company, department or individuals find themselves mired in what seemed to be a great idea gone bad.

Lists and outlines have served us well all of our lives, in fact most of us couldn't have functioned up to now without them. They work as well as they do because they share an important element with mind mapping—writing things down. Setting goals and tasks to paper engages a commitment process and provides review materials for later reference. That is where the similarity between mind maps and lists ends. Lists are still the best way to store some kinds of information—like directories, client lists, accounts payable and receivable etc., anything that benefits from sequential ordering—and mind maps are best for situations that call for prioritizing and making associations among groups of topics.

One problem inherent in listing is our tendency to assume a hierarchy of importance based on order of appearance from the top of the list down. This is shown, and even reinforced, by our expressions... "put this at the top of the list." Lists are more difficult to scan and do not provide the expansive, thought provoking characteristics of a mind map's visual stimulation, global overview and instant prioritization.

YOUR CALENDAR: 9 TO 5 AND IN-BETWEEN

Mind maps are the ideal supplement to calendars, lists and other tracking systems. They may or may not be a total replacement, depending on our ways of working. Calendars are essential for scheduling—putting the activities of days, weeks and months in chronological order—unless we have mastered the art of being in two or three places simultaneously.

Mind maps glue our days together, helping us to fill the gaps between scheduled tasks with planned activity for more effective use of discretionary time. But what about those wall-to-wall days, when it makes little sense to plan discretionary activity? Even then a glance at a mind map can reveal certain tasks that will take just a moment...

a phone call to expedite a certain event or a quick map of tomorrow's highlights, for example...and keep us functioning at full speed.

We all use mind maps whether we write them down or not. On days which require a less than frantic pace, we mentally sort and select priorities in mind map fashion. But when an emergency arises and we drop everything to deal with it, we often find ourselves in that dazed frame of mind known as "brain-fry." If we watch the habits of the Wildebeest on the Serengeti Plain, we see that when they are grazing, stress level is about as low as it gets for a Wildebeest. When a pride of lions attacks and the herd breaks into a full stampede, stress reaches near maximum levels. If a member of the herd is caught by the lions because of age, injury, or whatever, the herd will stop and begin grazing again, even though the lions may be feasting on a relative only yards away. Stress immediately plummets to its original level.

When we face tension in the workplace, we find our stress level rising only to have it stay high when the cause of the tension is removed. Without a mind map to reference we might wander about aimlessly for hours. With a mind map we can quickly scan it and answer the sacred time management question, "what is the best, most effective use of my time right now." In answering this question we factor in all the variables of how long each item takes—is there a lot of set up time, does it require a lot of creativity, and what is my mental state? It may be that we feel so frazzled the only thing we can do is go graze, or maybe we can run an important errand to renew a license that would take 45 minutes whether we are at our best or not. By accomplishing something productive we quickly become calm and re-energized to take on the more difficult tasks. A mind map then provides relief for our sizzled circuits, enabling us to focus on our next priority or choose a less-demanding action from our day's topics. It's surprising how fast we can snap back using a mind map for guidance, rather than coasting in a daze that can set up a spiral of reduced momentum for the rest of the day.

THE BEST LAID PLANS... LAID TO REST 'TIL TOMORROW?

We have all had days where we carefully plan our activities only to be swept up in a non-stop series of unplanned events. Emergency sessions, phone calls, drop-in conversations and chance meetings at the copy machine all add up to five o'clock and wondering where the day went. While it may be tempting to simply change the date on our daily mind map and start over tomorrow, a review of the items will invariably show some accomplishment related to our planned activities. Many of the same people and project items we schedule will surface during the course of the day. With a mind map prepared in advance these instances become opportunities to advance our agenda items.

Our map triggers the mental processes that encourage us to access our needs during a conversation or meeting within the flow of the exchange, and it doesn't seem to require any special effort.

Contrast this with the scenario where a visitor leaves your office and steps into an elevator just as you recall an item on your agenda, and you are faced with a game of phone tag for a day or more.

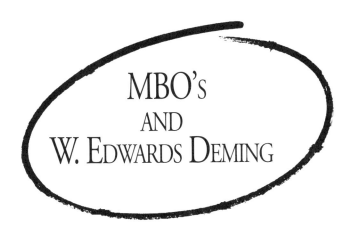

MBO'S
AND
W. EDWARDS DEMING

Dr. Deming's 11th point says " Eliminate 'Management By Objectives.' Eliminate management by numbers and numerical goals. Substitute leadership." At the risk of running contrary to the master of Quality, I believe the problem has not been in setting goals and objectives, but in setting the wrong objectives by focusing on short term profits. In addition, MBO's inflexibility has rendered it virtually useless as a tool in accomplishing any plan. It is rare that these MBO's are revised evenly quarterly, and this is simply too late for taking corrective action. The Plan/Do/Study/Act recommended by Deming is a form of setting goals and then revisiting and revising them as results warrant.

All of us have experienced the power of a deadline, like when we have to bring every project to some sort of completion so we can take that two-week vacation. Goals set up a structural tension that propel us to act and help our subconscious work on tasks even as we sleep. A twenty-year Stanford study showed that only 3 percent of Americans set clearly defined goals and those 3 percent earned ten times the amount of income as the average for all Americans.

Many quality experts talk of the tools of Quality. The most often mentioned include affinity diagrams, cause and effect diagrams, Pareto diagrams, control charts, and other statistical tools. The purpose of all of these tools is to array information in such a way as to enhance knowledge. Mind mapping also does this, and has many other applications that these tools do not fit.

STUCK IN
OVERDRIVE...
HEADED FOR
OVERLOAD

Folks with a severe random orientation often have a difficult time staying with any element of a project long enough to guarantee its satisfactory resolution. They are constantly racing past the present and on to the next step, which is perceived as much more important, until they get there. Once we start on any phase of a project, its importance seems secondary to other yet-to-be-addressed concerns. This behavior gives associates a message of impatience and non-importance which can damage team efforts, as well as contributing to our own hypertension.

It's often said that there is never enough time to do something right, but there is always time to do it over. A mind map is a great reminder of the big picture, helping random types recognize the whole as the sum of its parts, and the importance of each step on the way to a goal.

Every day consists of an array of activities, and focused effort yields a cumulative effect essential to the success of any endeavor. When our minds are two hours ahead of our current actions, we blow the present and never really get to the future. Slowing down via mind mapping allows us to focus on right now, do what needs to be done, and devote the same relaxed attention to our next step when the time is right.

NINE OUT OF TEN
DOCTORS
RECOMMEND...

Psychologists have identified poor communication as a leading cause of stress, and mind maps can play a big role in its reduction. Mapping goals and objectives provides a vehicle for us to analyze our activities and communicate them to others. Accurate information flows in as many directions as necessary when others can "read our minds" and leave guesswork out of the loop.

Using a mind map as a time management tool not only increases productivity through better organization and prioritization, it also facilitates the relaxed attention necessary to work at optimum efficiency.

A mind map's ability to generate more

creative and complete solutions to problems increases self-esteem while reducing fear, worry and guilt. So the next time you suffer an anxiety attack, make a mind map—it just might go away.

MAPS RECAPPED

Using mind maps is the only way to appreciate what they can help you accomplish, and how easily they can do it. If you haven't done one yet, or read the end of this section first, you don't know what you're missing. Pick a central topic, use a hub and spoke format to connect related ideas captured in balloons at the end of the spokes. The simple act of writing it down, along with the visual display will trigger a string of benefits that can only be appreciated by experience.

MANAGEMENT BY COMMUNICATION— MBO's REVISITED

The setting of goals and objectives is a personal and management practice that has been around since prehistoric man sketched an animal on a cave wall before going out to hunt. In the late 1960's and early '70s, a host of books and seminars elevated the process to an art-form of sorts under the heading "Management By Objectives," commonly referred to as MBO's.

The time has come to introduce Management By Communication, which can be described as an evolution of content and a revolution of style, when compared to traditional Management By Objectives. Management By Communication can greatly enhance an existing MBO system, salvage a flagging one, or rise from the wreckage of an

MBO program that has collapsed under its own weight.

Management By Communication provides a system of management that flexes with the styles of individual managers, and is more responsive to the high rate of change necessary in today's business environment.

KEEP THE BABY...
NOT THE
BATH WATER

A quick review of the positive aspects of MBO's may be in order at this point. The basic idea is to write down all goals and objectives to be accomplished over a time-specific interval, usually a year, and review periodically, hopefully every quarter. The process has several advantages, stimulating participants to consider activities in addition to basic administrative tasks, and to take on projects that might not otherwise be attempted. Goal-setting is in and of itself an action step through the commitment process.

MBO's also entail a tracking system to measure progress against stated objectives and desired timeframes. This step is critical since it prevents management plans from gathering dust in a desk drawer.

MANAGEMENT
BY OBJECTIVES...
OR BY
RESISTANCE?

Any movement, regardless of how progressive, is bound to meet some resistance. Resistance to MBO's often occurs in administration and operations. In the corporate environment, the writing and phrasing of the goals and objectives becomes a sensitive, therefore laborious, issue. The investment required in preparing and amending the initial document is usually lengthy and requires a high degree of structure and detail.

Reviewing the MBO is often difficult since objectives are spread out over multiple pages, and documentation will often focus on specific details, rather than selection and prioritization of projects. Because of the time and effort required to update MBO's, they are revised infrequently—quarterly, semi-annually or perhaps only annually. The quarterly option is by far the preferred solution when viewed from the perspective of responding to and implementing change. However, the time and effort involved make this a difficult choice, and resolution to unforeseen situations is usually accomplished without reference to the MBO document.

Change, therefore, propels the MBO system into de facto obsolescence. Any subsequent periodic reviews rely on MBO information that is invalid, outdated or currently irrelevant.

One probable result is frustration with the MBO process, with managers making decisions based on individual perception of current demand. Another occurrence is a suspension of reality and discussion of what should have been. In this case the MBO is viewed as "the Law," and its failure ascribed to something wrong with events "out there."

Priorities are wont to change with shifting situations, and since restructuring priorities means redrafting the entire MBO, it often suffers from benign neglect. Under a cumbersome system, the course of least resistance wins out, and outdated MBO statements gather dust while emergent situations are taken care of. Instead of being a daily guide to corporate direction, it becomes a collection of outdated long-term desires.

FROM CONFUSION TO COMMUNICATION

Mind mapping offers a vehicle that captures the planning benefits of traditional Management By Objectives, while maintaining the advantages of flexibility, speed and immediate response to change.

Instead of formally drafting a management goals and objectives, a mission statement, and explaining their relativity, it is only necessary to mind map them. This eliminates a lot of words that are truly irrelevant to action, and a lot of time spent finding just the right style and phraseology to represent management philosophy. When communication is done via mind map, only relevant action items are subject to interpretation, and there is time to convey corporate culture and style face-to-face, which is a much better way in the first place.

Depending on corporate structure, Management By Communication allows vital interaction between levels of management and production, and facilitates two-way communication. It might work like this: Managers at each level mind map yearly goals and objectives, with spin-off maps covering quarterly periods. Individual employees are asked to map individual goals and objectives that will help to achieve those of the company and their departments.

Information flows both ways in a series of meetings, where management can compare and adjust vertical and lateral departmental goals within the organization, and supervisors compare and adjust individual goals to correspond with the company objectives as a whole.

Since everyone involved gets a look at the big picture as it unfolds, there is an opportunity for suggestions and ideas that might not otherwise be explored. Since mind maps only take a minute or so to prepare, communication between decision-makers and decision- implementers does not get bogged down in detail. Priorities can be discussed, set, quantified and revised with a minimum of fuss, and everyone involved gets a clear picture of what is important—right now.

Monthly updates of quarterly mind maps take just a few moments, regardless of an individual's function. And the presence of the mind map system of management also encourages status reports on-the-fly, because maps can be easily reworked to fit changing situations. Teamwork is empha-sized, and management has created a feedback loop that highlights progress and problems in time to respond to them. Managers have all the information they need to communicate effectively with superiors and subordinates, and identify difficulties as well as opportunities at the earliest possible moment. A picture of the cycle is shown on the following page.

MANAGERS	INDIVIDUALS	MANAGERS & INDIVIDUALS JOINTLY
PROVIDE MISSION STATEMENT & TOP LEVEL GOALS		
MIND MAP GOALS & OBJECTIVES FOR INDIVIDUALS (REFERENCE ONLY)	MIND MAP GOALS & OBJECTIVES	REVIEW & REVISE ANNUAL GOALS & OBJECTIVES
MIND MAP 3-MONTH GOALS & OBJECTIVES FOR INDIVIDUALS (REFERENCE ONLY)	MIND MAP 3-MONTH GOALS & OBJECTIVES	REVIEW & REVISE 3-MONTH GOALS & OBJECTIVES
MIND MAP NEXT 3 MONTH'S GOALS & OBJECTIVES FOR INDIVIDUALS— DROPPING PAST MONTH & ADDING NEXT (REFERENCE ONLY)	REVIEW PAST MONTH & MIND MAP NEXT 3 MONTH'S GOALS & OBJECTIVES	REVIEW PAST MONTH & REVISE 3 MONTH'S GOALS & OBJECTIVES

Annual goals and the plans generated to achieve them can become a corporate millstone without frequent review. As any given year progresses, the likelihood that January's projections for the ultimate success story are still on target becomes increasingly remote.

With Management By Communication in place, a review of the big picture can occur as a matter of need or interest at any time—without requiring a major overhaul. It's simply a matter of coordinating the existing information contained in quarterly maps (which have been reviewed monthly) and updating the yearly mind map to reflect situational changes.

A comparison of the results achieved throughout the year to the projections of the original plan can be very illuminating. It's entirely possible that the year's most significant achievement might not have been part of the original mind map. Other projects may have lost urgency or even relevance, replaced by opportunities impossible to predict when objectives were first formulated.

In addition to becoming an accurate history of goals and key elements in their accomplishment as the year unfolds, mind maps indicate trends that can increase forecasting accuracy, and provide important information relevant to how a company or department functions.

A Performance Appraisal Is Not Reality

The interactive aspect of Management By Communication is the real clincher. By structuring monthly meetings with participants to discuss quarterly mind maps, managers ensure essential communication that includes information exchange, progress reports, emerging problems, new opportunities, coaching and mentoring, performance feedback and participant recognition.

Using the mind map as the agenda helps the discussion stay on track and we are less apt to spend 80% of the meeting talking about the little things and leaving some important items out altogether or quickly brushing on them because we ran out of time.

By sharing meeting results with the entire team, everyone feels that they know what is going on, what's new, what's hot and what's not. And no one burns midnight oil on tabled or terminated projects.

EVENT MANAGER
OR
TIME ACCOUNTANT?

We all have a tendency as managers to fall into an accounting trap, spending our time accounting for ourselves and our departments, rather than managing to lead our charges to greater accomplishments. When we stop to think about it, we don't manage time, we only structure events within its reference. It's always asked "Don't all these meetings waste a lot of time?" While monthly management meetings do require a time and energy commitment from each manager, managers get paid to manage, and Management By Communication fits the job description of a manager far better than the many administrative and reporting tasks that often eat up a manager's time.

In terms of time expended, meeting preparation time is relatively little, compared to the time utilized exchanging vital information. And that process itself is more efficient, since mind maps provide an agenda that keeps meetings on the right track.

And while we're at it...

Meetings are a fact of business life, and can be an effective way of passing on information and reaching consensus for making decisions. They can just as often be a pain in the timeframe. They are frequently held too often, last too long and involve too many people. Rather than furthering objectives, these kinds of meetings waste time, create boredom and reduce momentum.

A consistent reason for poor meetings is the want of an effective agenda. When a mind map is used to prepare and communicate an agenda, participants begin with a clear overview of a particular meeting's content and objectives. Mind mapping a proposed meeting allows for easy sequencing of action items and time allotments to ensure that twenty-minute meetings last twenty minutes, instead of turning into marathon sessions.

Key personnel can plan their time efficiently and be excused if necessary once their specific needs and interests are met. Asking each participant to mind map their own mini-agendas within the overall meeting framework will provide clear accountability for reporting and proposed actions when preparing minutes and attending to follow-up.

With today's managers spending anywhere from 10-to-50 percent of their productive time in meetings, improved meeting technique can be leveraged into significant benefits.

Effective meetings with clear agendas send a strong signal to team members that their time and energy are valued by the organization.

Management By Communication is an ideal complement to Tom Peters' strategy of Management by Walking Around. Rather than sitting in an office chained to administrative detail, a manager is actively engaged in face-to-face communication with all project or department members—giving and receiving information necessary to getting the job done.

Management By Communication continually provides big picture awareness to everyone involved, and participants stay motivated, knowing exactly what they need to do to maximize team effectiveness. Decisions are made when they need to be, based on accurate information that supports big picture results.

Having a mind map of our daily plans assures the productivity of those wanderings by making sure we pay attention to the things that are truly important and timely, before we get caught up in the communications with emerging priorities that can so quickly take us off our charted course.

MBCDEFG:
MORE THAN
ALPHABET SOUP

Management By Communication sets up a system that will stand the tests of time and pressure. Good management was once accurately defined as "getting people to want to do what we want them to do." By encouraging the participation of team members in setting, amending and achieving goals and objectives an entire series of benefits is set in motion:

M – Multitudes of goals, objectives and strategies will be generated as each team member is stimulated to search for specific results.

B – By writing down goals and objectives, internal, as well as external, commitment takes place.

C – Communication is assured by the structure, which requires a review of progress.

D – Development of contingency or alternative plans is a natural by-product of progress reviews.

E – Effort is naturally stimulated by the joint process of negotiated goals and objectives.

F – Frequent review is facilitated by the ease and speed in which objectives can be revised.

G – Good performance is the norm as participants enjoy a sense of fulfillment as set goals are achieved on a regular basis.

It's a lot more than alphabet soup, it's just about all you can ask for in a management system.

A
BETTER
REPORT CARD

After twelve monthly review sessions at every level of responsibility in a given company, it becomes a mere formality to create management and employee appraisals. Anyone who takes part in performance reviews on either side of the desk knows how uncomfortable they can be without objective criteria. Mind maps will have provided all the content necessary for an accurate, in-depth performance review...a comparison of results versus mutually agreed upon expectations, along with the regular opportunity to revise those expectations in light of current conditions. At a personal level it is very gratifying for individuals to know that they are in step with management objectives, working to meet a mutual definition for success—and a great morale builder to know that efforts are duly recorded and rewarded.

THE FINAL STEP

Whether used in the business world, strictly in our personal lives, or in both, mind mapping is a tool that works and works well. Most of us have all arrived at this point in our lives without it and done all right. So there may be a natural resistance to try something new. We will have to displace an old habit and develop a new one. Experts say this takes, on average, twenty-one days.

Let's begin by making at least one mind map each day for the next three weeks and develop a positive addiction to this great tool. As a reminder, move your wastebasket, and each time you miss it, ask yourself if you did your mind map to day.

Happy mapping.

SHARE THIS DYNAMITE CONCEPT WITH A FRIEND OR ASSOCIATE.

Yes! Send me_____copy(ies) of *The 59-Second Mind Map,* @ $9.95 each ($11.95 Canadian), plus $3.50 for shipping and handling.

Washington residents add 82¢ sales tax.

Name_____

Address_____

City_____St_____Zip_____

Mail to:
Sound Communication
3633 Beach Drive S.W., Ste 402
Seattle, WA 98116-2750